My C.C.C. Days

Memories of the Civilian Conservation Corps

By
Frank C. Davis

2006
Parkway Publishers, Inc.
Boone, North Carolina

Library of Congress Cataloging-in-Publication Data

Davis, Frank C.
My C.C.C. days : Civilian Conservation Corps / by Frank
C. Davis.
p. cm.
Summary: "This book details the experiences of 18-year-old
Frank Davis, a native of Mebane, North Carolina, who joined
Civilian Conservation Corps. Davis was assigned to work in the
mountains of western North Carolina building trails"—Provided
by publisher.
ISBN-13: 978-1-933251-23-3
1. Civilian Conservation Corps (U.S.). Camp NP5 (Great
Smoky Mountains National Park, N.C. and Tenn.)—History. 2.
Davis, Frank C. 3. Civilian Conservation Corps (U.S.).
Company 411 (N.C.)—Officials and employees—Biography. I.
Title.

S932.N8D38 2006
333.75'160976889—dc22
2005026910

Book and Cover Design by: Terry Henry

The moving finger writes; and, having writ, moves on:
Nor all thy Piety nor Wit shall lure it back to cancel half a line,
Nor all thy Tears wash out a word of it.

Omar Khayyam

Table of Contents

Chapter One

Joining Up

On March 4, 1933, President Franklin D. Roosevelt took office. It was said that the lights in all the government buildings in Washington, D.C. burned all night that night. By 7:00 a.m. the next morning the Civilian Conservation Corps (C.C.C.) was off and running. It was the middle of the Great Depression and many young men could not find jobs, nor could they afford to go to college. The development of the C.C.C. was one solution to this unemployment problem. A young man had to be eighteen years of age to join the C.C.C. He was paid thirty dollars a month, of which twenty-five dollars was sent home to help his family, and he was allowed to keep five dollars for incidentals. In this way the boy's family also received aid.

One day in downtown Mebane, North Carolina, my hometown, I ran into a boyhood friend of mine. My friend asked, "How about going with me to join the C.C.C.? I don't want to go by myself."

The next day I drove my father to Reidsville, North Carolina, to his job interview. My father got the job and remained in Reidsville. On the way back home I went by the Alamance County Courthouse to get some information on joining the C.C.C. Although I walked in only to get information, I walked out signed up ready to leave the next day for Raleigh. When I arrived home, my mother flipped. She was losing her only child of 18 years.

The next morning we were driven to Raleigh, North Carolina, and there I, along with a number of boys from all over the state, was given a physical examination. Late that afternoon we were loaded into a railroad passenger car and the whole carload was taken to Fort Bragg, North Carolina, because the army was given the job of running the C.C.C. We arrived there about 2:00 a.m. the next morning.

Frank Davis while at Fort Bragg waiting to be assigned to a C.C.C. camp

We were ushered from the railroad car and into a mess hall where we were given doughnuts and coffee. We were then assigned the tents in which we were to live for the next two weeks. We were quartered, six men to a tent, with folding army cots and straw tick mattresses to sleep on. The next morning we were given another and more detailed physical examination.

We were issued mess kits and our meals were served in the mess hall. The cooks wore white shirts and pants and large white chef's hats. The food they served was good. It consisted of such things as ham and eggs, cereal, and milk and coffee to drink. The boys would eat until all the food was gone. I would sometimes go back for seconds and thirds in the chow line. One day the mess sergeant said to me, "Boy, don't you ever get enough to eat?" I answered, "Not that I can remember." Outside the mess hall there was a steel drum filled with water where we could wash our mess kits.

While at Fort Bragg, Frank donned a soldier's uniform and had his picture made.

Every morning we were assembled for roll call and were assigned a job for the day, never the same job every day. One day we were asked if anyone could handle horses. I volunteered—anything to get away from the pick and shovel. I think I had the meanest pair of horses on the post. They were hitched to a large two-wheeled dirt scoop. I had to drive them down into a large pit to scoop up a load of dirt. The horses were afraid of the tractor and I had a tough time controlling them. I then drove them out of the pit to a place where the dirt was dumped and spread. One day of this was enough for me. The next day and each day thereafter, I had a different job.

After two weeks at Fort Bragg, we were assigned to the camp where we were to serve during our stay in the C.C.C. We were divided up among several camps and I was sent to a different camp than my hometown friend. This created quite a furor. Boys were approaching the army sergeant and asking to trade assignments with others in order to stay with their hometown buddies. I'll never forget the sergeant's answer: "What the hell, what good are the people you've hung around with all your life? You can't borrow any money from them. Go meet new people and make new friends." He was right!

Chapter 2

My Journey There

When we left Fort Bragg for our assigned camp, we were again loaded into railroad passenger cars for the trip. It was late afternoon when we pulled out. The cars they used to haul us around were very old, probably pulled out of retirement, but they were comfortable. We rode all night, and the next day at daylight I looked out the window to find myself in the mountains. I was looking down into a valley and saw my first artesian well. It was spouting high into the air. I think it was somewhere around Old Fort, North Carolina. This was the first time for me and many of the other boys to see such high mountains. It was the highlight of the trip.

We arrived in Bryson City, North Carolina, around eight o'clock in the morning. There was a group of trucks waiting for

The men of Company 411, Camp NP5 in the Great Smoky Mountain National Park. The arrow points to Frank Davis.

us. The C.C.C. fellow in charge called the roll. After checking our names off the list, we were loaded on the trucks for our trip to the camp. This camp was about twenty-five miles away at a place near Smokemont, North Carolina, an area of the park called the Kephart Prong, about halfway between the Cherokee Indian Reservation and Newfound Gap. I had been assigned to Company 411, Camp NP5 in the Great Smoky Mountains National Park. I enjoyed the ride while taking in the mountain scenery.

A view of the CCC camp from up on the mountain.

When we arrived at the camp we were taken into the mess hall and given a meal. After that we had the rest of the day off. Because the camp was surrounded by tall mountains, some of the boys were compelled to climb a mountain, not realizing that behind that mountain was another higher than the first.

Chapter Three

Work in the C.C.C. Camp

For my first day at work in the C.C.C. Camp I was assigned to the trail crew. Our job was to build fire trails throughout the mountains to give access for firefighters to combat forest fires, and to build hiking trails for recreational use. At 8:00 a.m. we left the camp and started walking to the job. As the trail progressed, the work area became farther and farther from the camp. On this day we walked for three hours before reaching the work site. We worked for one hour and then stopped for lunch. Our lunches were brown bags picked up that morning when leaving the mess hall. They were all alike, of course, consisting of a baloney sandwich, a cheese sandwich, a peanut butter sandwich, and a jelly sandwich. Peanut butter and jelly were my favorite, so I traded my baloney sandwich and my cheese sandwich for another peanut butter and another jelly. Putting them together I had two extra thick peanut butter and jelly sandwiches.

One of the boys was assigned the job of water boy and his job was to keep the canteens filled. It was up to him to go somewhere and find water. Sometimes he would walk all over the mountain looking for water. One day our water boy got lost and it was the next day before he found his way back to camp. The higher you climbed the mountain the scarcer water became. It finally got down to a mere trickle.

After lunch we went back to work for a couple of hours and then had to start walking back to camp. The trip down the mountain was much faster than the trip up. Thank God for those heavy army issue shoes! Going down the trail, your feet would slide forward in your shoes and cramp your toes.

Luckily, my assignment to the trail crew came when they were going over previously built trails and cleaning them off. In the early days we had to carry blacksmith shop equipment up the trail to set up shop to keep the tools sharp.

One special crew was the dynamite crew. Unlike the road gang, who had jackhammers and air compressors for drilling holes for dynamite, the trail boys had to drill by hand. The dynamite crew was a three-man crew consisting of one man who held the long steel drill while the other two took turns driving the drill with sledgehammers. The man holding the drill was called the steel shaker. He had to turn the drill a quarter turn each time it was hit. He was the bravest, for heaven help him if one of the other two missed. After driving a while with the sledgehammers you graduated to the special steel-driving hammer. This hammer was like the sledgehammer save for a section between the handle and the hammerhead that was thin and flat. This was so that when you swung the hammer back you could turn the handle one-quarter turn and lay the flat side across your shoulder. This would allow the handle to bend and the weight of the head would bend

View of Newfound Gap and the new road built by the CCC boys.

the handle along the flat of your back. This would give the upswing more power to strike the drill. Of course, all this drilling was through stone, and my hat's off to these guys.

Upon leaving the trail crew, I was assigned to the road gang. A contractor had built a road from Cherokee, North Carolina, through the park to Gatlinburg, Tennesee. Our job was to slope the banks along the road from our camp up to Newfound Gap, which was the top of the mountain ridge that formed the line between North Carolina and Tennessee. We were also responsible for building walls along the roads to serve as guard rails and for building overlooks which would provide a place for travelers to pull off the road and enjoy the scenic views.

The contractor who built the highway left cuts through the mountain ridges with vertical banks. During the winter months and after heavy rains there would be landslides that blocked the road. We would slope these cuts back and plant vegetation to prevent further erosion.

The work was all pick, shovel and wheelbarrow. We would dig into the side of the mountain, loosening dirt and rock that would slide down to the road below. There, two guys would shovel the dirt into a wheelbarrow and a third guy would push it over to the shoulder of the road and dump it to create the overlooks.

Sometimes the wheelbarrow load would consist of a huge rock. When we pushed it over to the shoulder to dump it, the wheelbarrow would get away

While working on the road our job was to slope the banks along the new road being built up to Newfound Gap. The work was all done manually with pick, shovels, and wheelbarrows.

from us and roll down the mountain. We would then have to crawl down the mountainside and drag it back up and at the same time watch out for other rocks coming over the shoulder.

When we would leave camp every morning after breakfast we would take our mess kits with us because lunch would be served up on the road. A mess kit looks like a frying pan that folds and contains a knife, fork, spoon, and a little cup. At lunchtime a dump truck would be sent back to camp to pick up the cooks and their "field kitchen." The field kitchen consisted of large containers of whatever food was being served that day. We would line up with our mess kits and pass by the mess cans where the cooks would serve our food. We would eat like we worked – hard. After lunch the cooks would load their field kitchen back in the truck and we would go back to work.

Sometimes we would tie ropes to trees higher up the mountainside, fashion a little seat on the other end and swing like a pendulum back and forth while digging into the mountainside with a pickaxe. The road itself was kept open for tourist traffic. One day as a car drove by a small kid yelled, "Look, there's a mean one, they've got him tied."

Chapter Four

The New Power Shovel

The big power shovel the Park Service brought in for excavation changed our work load.

The National Park Service eventually bought a big power shovel for excavation into the side of the mountain. It came in on a railroad flat car via a narrow gauge railroad that ran into the little ghost town of Ravens Ford. Ravens Ford was the site of the mill that sawed all the timber that was cut from the North Carolina side of the mountains. Later, this area and part of Tennessee were condemned by the government and made part of the Great Smoky Mountains National Park. The Tennessee side of the park was still virgin timber.

The company that built the power shovel sent a representative to Ravens Ford, to unload the shovel and drive it up to the camp. The camp superintendent, Mr. E. J. Rosser, and I went down to Ravens Ford to meet him. The company man unloaded the shovel from the flat car and drove it to the camp, a distance of several miles.

The shovel traveled on two large caterpillar tracks. The track driving gears, both right and left, could be disengaged separately by controls on the inside of the shovel. But there were no brake controls inside. They were on the outside. I had to walk along in front and apply each brake by hand so the shovel could navigate the crooked road to the camp.

When the shovel finally reached the work site our workload changed considerably. We had, if I recall correctly, acquired about five or six trucks. One was a Chevrolet stake body truck and the remaining were dump trucks, Fords, Dodges, and one White. Drivers were assigned to the trucks and the park service hired an operator to run the shovel. The dump truck drivers would back their trucks into position so that the shovel operator, after digging into the side of the mountain, could swing the shovel boom around and drop the dipper load into the dump truck, then swing back to the mountain for another load. The truck driver would have to keep his eye on the shovel operator, who would give him a signal when the truck was sufficiently loaded. The driver would then pull out and drive to the overlook site that was being built and dump the load of dirt. We had a caterpillar type tractor there that would push the dirt over the side of the road. The tractor driver was an assigned C.C.C. boy.

Ravens Ford had once been a lumber town with a big lumber mill. The town had a little narrow gauge railroad pulled by a little steam engine that ran back up into the mountains and hauled the logs down to town. By the time the C.C.C. began, Ravens Ford was almost a ghost town. About the only other thing still in operation in the town was the post office. Most of the other buildings had been torn down and their lumber was used to build the C.C.C. Camps.

Some of the equipment used to build the road to Newfound Gap.

Building the road to Newfound Gap.

Chapter Five

A Change of Duty

Frank Davis in front of the old wooden grease rack.

One day, as I was returning to camp from work on the road, I noticed a guy working on a truck on the old wooden grease rack that had been built for servicing the camp trucks. I went over and talked to him and he said that he was the camp mechanic but he was leaving in a few weeks. In those days you were allowed to stay in the service for only two years. I told the camp mechanic that I had worked as a helper in an automobile repair shop for a while before joining the C.C.C.

My experience in a automobile reapir shop came after graduating from high school. I could not afford college and there were others in my graduating class in the same boat. The high school superintendent offered to teach a class in first year college math each school day morning. This was very generous on his part as his duties as superintendent did not require this. He did it in case some of us might make it to college later. So after graduating from high school in May of 1932, I would go back to school for one hour each morning beginning in September 1932.

Each morning, after class, I would go by a local furniture company plant and ask for a job. Each day the foreman would say, "No, we don't need anybody." I would be back again the next day and the next. One day he said, "Boy, I told you yesterday we don't need anybody."

I said, "Yes, I know, but that was yesterday and this is today." Finally one day he said, "Boy, it looks like the only way I'm going to get rid of you is to give you a job." I said, "That's what I had in mind."

The job was for ten hours a day and paid ten cents an hour. This gave me one dollar a day. Later, in compliance with President Roosevelt's "New Deal" ruling, the workday was shortened to eight hours. Then, due to a lack of furniture orders, the workweek was shortened to three days—two dollars and forty cents a week. Sometimes this would be paid in scrip, a piece of paper that was good in only three stores in town. It was time for me to go.

There was a man in town who worked for an automobile repair shop. I would ride my old motorcycle in there sometimes and borrow tools from him to work on my rig to keep it running. I had traded my bicycle for the rig with one dollar to boot. It had no state license tag on it; I figured if I rode it on country roads only and stayed off the state highways the highway patrol would not bother me.

One day the automobile mechanic said he would let me work for him and pay me what he could afford when he had a good week. He was working on commission. I spent many happy hours working with him—this was the kind of work I loved. My father had been an automobile mechanic in his early days. It kind of ran in the family. Finally came my entrance into the C.C.C. and now – back to the grease rack.

I applied for the camp mechanic job, got it, and thank goodness that meant no more pick and shovel. My job was to see that all the trucks got out on the job every morning. I had the rest of the day pretty much to myself except that I had to go out each day and grease the tractor. A truck driver would come into camp, pick me up and take me out to the work site. One day while on the job I needed a leather washer to repair the grease gun that I was using. Being miles away from anywhere and stuck on the side of a mountain, I took my pocket knife out of my pocket, cut a piece of leather out of my shoe and made a washer. I thought that I was being pretty resourceful but when I got back to camp I caught the devil from the supply clerk for ruining a pair of shoes. I said to him, "I have to keep things rolling."

When the trucks came in at the close of each workday I had to service them. This meant greasing, changing oil, and whatever

Frank Davis and friends working on a truck.

Frank Davis trying out one of the trucks on which he was working.

Frank Davis with truck on old wooden grease rack.

else that was needed. I managed to be finished by chow time for I loved to eat.

The National Park Service employed a supervisory mechanic who was in charge of a small shop in the nearby town of Bryson City, North Carolina. The trucks would be taken there if they needed major work done on them. He would also tour all the surrounding camps in the area in a specially equipped pickup truck containing tools, welding equipment, and other items, and check all the trucks in the area. Sometimes he would come by, pick me up, and take me with him. He was a great guy. He always carried a fishing pole with him. When we would pass a likely looking fishing hole, we would stop and try it out. Frankly, I think he did this more for my benefit than for his.

One morning as I walked up to the top of the hill to see the truck off when the camp superintendent nabbed me and said,"You are going to be the tractor driver today."

"What?" I replied. "Me? A tractor driver?"

"Yes, you," he said. "I've been watching you and you can handle it."

I guess that was because on weekends they would bring the caterpillar tractor into camp and I would have to service it, grease it, and change the oil. Afterward I would crank it up and practice driving it. I would see how steep I could climb the mountain with the tractor, whirl around and do all kinds of things. I enjoyed

Frank Davis working on a truck.

myself but it caught up with me.

I was picked to drive that day because the regular driver had to go into town for a dental appointment. The Army would send dental doctors around periodically to check our teeth. If you needed treatment you were sent into town for it to be done.

That day proved to be a memorable one for me. We were building a road through the Cherokee Indian Reservation to a place called "Round Bottom" where there were plans to build another C.C.C. Camp. The road followed a former horse trail

On weekends the caterpillar tractor would be brought into camp and I would have to service it. Afterward I would crank it up and practice driving it. I would see how steep I could climb the mountain with it. One day the regular driver had to go into town. The camp superintendent said, "You are going to be the tractor driver today".

Frank Davis with tractor used in building road through the national park.

that was used by the horseback riding mailman who delivered mail once a week.

Old "Coon Hunter" Day was in charge of the project and he was a man who could get it done. The first half of the day proved to be easy. All I had to do was move the tractor forward a few yards every now and then because we were crushing rock that had been left in piles along the side of the road. The tractor had a portable rock crusher in tow that was driven by a power take-off shaft from the tractor. We would spread the crushed rock over the surface of the road as we progressed.

After lunch Coon Hunter said to me, "I want you to move the rock crusher up the hill there and back it up to the edge of the cliff. We are going to crush rock and let it fall into the trucks parked below." That was easier said than done, but I had to get it done. This very nervous tractor driver accomplished the task and things went along very well.

The next day the regular tractor driver was back on the job but I stayed on a while longer servicing and keeping the rock crusher going. One day while working on this project we passed an Indian school and I was fascinated with the Indian children there. They would hide behind trees and peep out at us. They also played a kind of a ball game that I had never seen before. They threw the ball and caught it with a kind of paddle that had a hole in its face to which was attached a small net. The ball would go through the hole and into the net. To me it looked like a combination of our baseball game and our football game. They would try to make it to the goal line without being caught holding the ball. Years later I would go back to the reservation to attend one of their Indian fairs, and there I watched the grownups play the same game, which I learned was called stickball.

Before leaving Coon Hunter, let me mention this. Another time, while working along the road to Newfound Gap, the road was blocked with the power shovel. A truck showed up loaded with very heavy bags of cement headed for the contractor who was building the road from Newfound Gap out to Clingman's Dome. The truck driver asked that the shovel be moved. He was told to drive around on the overlook that we were building. Being afraid that the soft dirt would not support his heavy truckload of cement bags, he refused. Coon Hunter told him that he had supervised the building of that overlook and that it would hold him. After much argument the truck driver gave in, pulled around, and went on his way. Coon Hunter turned to his straw boss Harvey and said, "Aye, God, Harve, I guess I'm a hundred years old when it comes to experience." I have to agree and I take my hat off to him.

Chapter Six

Returning to Camp After Leave Time

When I would go home on leave I can't recall exactly how I would make the trips, but I'll never forget the return trips.

On the day that I was to return I would go down to the Mebane railroad depot and purchase my ticket. The train would come through town that night around two a.m. My mother would sit up with me until 1:30 a.m. when I would leave to catch the train.

The depot would be closed but the station agent, Mr. Ed Farrell, a distant cousin of mine, would set the signal for the train to stop and leave a fire in the pot-bellied stove in the waiting room, which never closed. The train would stop and I would be the only passenger getting on. After a thirty minute ride I would arrive at Greensboro and there change trains for Salisbury, where I would change again for Asheville. It would be daylight by this time and I would board another train for Sylva, the final leg of the railroad trip.

The journey from Asheville to Sylva would take almost as long as the entire first part of the trip. At one point along the way the train would stop and the conductor would walk down a path to a house and deliver a newspaper.

I would always arrange my trip so that I would arrive in Sylva on a Saturday because there would be a truck in town that night bringing a load of C.C.C. boys for a night on the town. The truck would depart around 11 p.m. for the trip back to camp and I would be aboard. Those were the days!

Chapter Seven

The Schoolhouse

At one point on the "Round Bottom Road" project there was a two-shift operation set up for truck drivers. One morning after breakfast the second shift drivers were lolling around practicing being lazy, when the army lieutenant noticed them and mustered the group to form a campground clean-up team.

As they were working on the grounds down from the top of the hill, where a small building that we called the "schoolhouse" stood, here came Ed Williams, who we called "King Kong". We didn't give him that name; he brought it with him. King Kong was the C.C.C. boy who was assigned the job of taking care of and operating the schoolhouse. It was an all-day and part-of-the-night job, for it was there that a lot of the boys spent their evenings reading books, magazines, and listening to the radio. As King Kong walked by the work crew he said, "Boys, this college life is killing me!" The lieutenant replied, "Williams, grab a rake and fall in here with these guys!" A few minutes later while raking his heart out King Kong said, "Boys, it's not the college life that's killing me, it's all this work on the campus!"

The little building was called the schoolhouse because it was there that small classes would be taught on various subjects, often times by other C.C.C. boys who had expertise in certain trades. I even taught a class, for a short while, on automotive maintenance.

The camp tried to do everything they could to help the young men learn a trade, and many did. A good friend of mine started by driving a truck in the camp and later worked his way up. When he left the camp and returned to his hometown, he got a job with a construction company. The company had just purchased a large power shovel and my friend was the one in the company to operate it. By working hard and applying what he had learned in the C.C.C. Camp, he eventually became a full partner with the company. Another young man who began working in the camp as a cook later became a cook in the Merchant Marines.

One day a U.S. Army Chaplain came by to see us and put on a demonstration of hypnotism for us in the schoolhouse. He brought one of the boys under his spell and told him it was freezing cold in there. The boy started shivering and we kept handing him coats to put on. Then he was told that it was very warm in the place and he started sweating and shedding the coats. Next he was told he had a severe toothache. That was a mistake. Aside from groaning he came out with some very bad profanity. The chaplain quickly brought him out of it and never hypnotized us again.

Chapter Eight

My First Dance

I spent many happy hours in the little schoolhouse listening to the latest big dance bands, such as Guy Lombardo and Wayne King. I think it was there that I developed a desire to start attending the dances that we often had at the camp.

I had never been to a dance and never danced with a girl. Not only I, but several other guys in the camp were in the same boat, so we got together and practiced dancing with one another.

A dance was coming up and we made an agreement that if we didn't dance with a girl that night we would have to run through a belt line the next day. The belt line was a double line of boys with their belts in their hands who would take a whack at you as you ran through. I had no intention of doing that.

So on the night of the dance I stood on the sideline with a mouth full of chewing gum, chewing it a mile a minute to ease my nervousness. One of the boys ahead of me had had his face slapped on his first try.

I figured if I had to go, I would go first class, so I picked out a girl with long beautiful black hair and broke in on her partner. I probably had a wrestler's hold on her while still chewing, when suddenly I noticed a strange taste in my mouth. My chewing gum was caught in her hair! I immediately stopped chewing and continued dancing with locked jaws, hoping someone would break on me. When they finally did I opened my mouth, backed off, and hit the door, headed for the barracks. In spite of this chewing gum incident, I eventually became a fairly good dancer and enjoyed the later dances held at the camp.

WHERE: Company 1211, CCC Smokemont, N. C.

WHEN : Friday, May the 24th, 1935.

WHAT : Informal Dance.

WHO : YOU (and your friends)

9:00 till ??????   Refreshments !!!!!!!!

Invitation to Miss Elizabeth Sherrill to a dance at the C.C.C. camp.

The members of Company 414, Civilian Conservation
Corps cordially invite you to attend a dance at

      CAMP WILLIAM H. THOMAS
        Smokemont, N.C.

Time 8:30 until 1:30, Friday night, February 1st.

        MUSIC BY-
 "THE BUCCANEERS ORCHESTRA" Ashville, N.C.

You are requested to present this card for entrance

                KSH/

Postcard to Elizabeth Sherrill

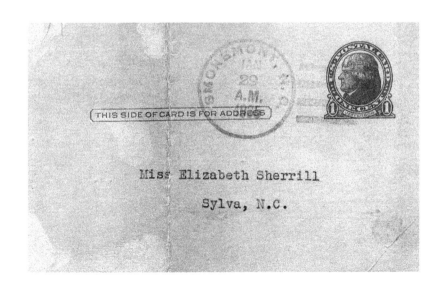

THIS SIDE OF CARD IS FOR ADDRESS

Miss Elizabeth Sherrill

Sylva, N.C.

We would also sometimes have orchestras that came out from neighboring cities to play for the dances. There is one in particular that I will always remember because it stemmed from the following childhood event.

When I was a small kid, around four or five years old, my folks lived across the street from a Mr. & Mrs. Daley in Charlotte, North Carolina. They had a daughter, Neta Daley, my same age with whom I played. We moved away from Charlotte when I was still a kid but I had an aunt there who kept us posted on news of the Daley family. I knew that Neta had begun teaching tap dancing.

On this particular night the orchestra had come all the way from Asheville, North Carolina, where they were playing for a resort hotel. They brought their floorshow with them. For the introduction of the floorshow the orchestra leader said, "Now we bring you two tap dancers, Miss Neta and Miss Mona Daley, from Charlotte, North Carolina." I said, "My God that's her!" I would not have known her or she me.

When they finished their performance and went into the makeshift dressing room (our barber shop) to change costumes, I posted myself outside the door to meet Neta when she came out. Was she ever surprised! We danced together the rest of the evening. After the dance there was a little social in the mess hall and I sat with the orchestra. Neta invited me to visit her at their performance in Asheville, but that was a little out of my league. It would be several years before I saw her again.

Chapter Nine

Life in the Barracks

I had been assigned a bunk (army folding cot) next to a boy named Edison Weatherly. We called him "Stormy", though Stormy Weather was more appropriate. Stormy had built himself a little one-tube battery operated radio which didn't work. I had built radios when I was in high school, so I agreed to see what I could do with it. I soon found the trouble. Stormy had used a tube of something called plastic solder made with some kind of cement and hand-powdered aluminum. The plastic solder was not a good conductor of electrical current. I brought down a blowtorch and soldering iron from the

Frank (left) and good friend Stormy Weather.

so-called camp workshop and re-soldered the connections using electrical solder. The set worked well - sometimes too well. Stormy had run wires a few bunks down the line so a friend could listen to the radio with earphones. At ten o'clock each night we had lights out and we were supposed to be in bed. One night, after ten o'clock, the lieutenant came through on an inspection tour and shined his flashlight on the friend's bunk and the fellow sat straight up in bed with the headphones on. Stormy's secret was out, but he was allowed to keep his radio. I later "confiscated" a battery from one of the trucks to keep it working. This could have been a break for Stormy because he was later transferred to Fort Oglethorpe.

Along with the army cots we were issued to sleep on, we were also issued the same number of blankets. Sometimes when it got very, very cold, some of us would pool our covers and double up – sometimes even triple up. We would push two cots together, side by side, and spread out three sets of covers. We would take turns being the third man who would have to sleep in the middle on the cot edge poles. Thankfully that didn't happen very often. Each barracks had two wood stoves – one at each end of the building. There was a night watchman whose job it was to keep the fires burning during the wintertime. But on the nights that the temperature would drop below zero, we had to be creative to keep from freezing.

We didn't have much in the way of clothes, and all we had were army issue. If we had a date with a girl in town we would borrow clothes from one another. For example, a young man might borrow pants from one guy and a shirt from another. On

Home, sweet home.

special occasions like Thanksgiving and Christmas, the camp would provide a big dinner in the main halls and we were allowed to invite someone from out of town, such as a girlfriend. We looked forward to these events because they meant good food and good company, but sharing clothes became more difficult because everyone wanted to look good.

Photo of napkin from Thanksgiving Dinner 1935 (found in an old scrapbook). Listed on the napkin is the menu and the names of all the men in Company 411.

Chapter Ten

Life With The Animals

Not only were we happy in our camp, but a number of animals were also happy there. One night I awoke smelling a terrible odor. Something had encountered a skunk under our barracks floor. The skunk did a number on whatever it was and sprayed it good. That terrible odor, of course, came right up through the cracks in the floor. Apparently I was the only victim, for I looked around me and everyone else was still sound asleep. I got up, moved to the other end of the camp, and breathed fresh air till daylight.

We had two German police dogs in the camp. We loved them very much, and they loved all of us. One day, somewhere, somehow, they jumped a skunk. The skunk did a number on them, spraying them good. For the next week when they would approach us to be petted, we would chase them away. I hope they understood, but I doubt it.

One night as the night watchman was walking past the mess hall he noticed what looked like someone digging into the garbage can. He walked over, held up his lantern to see who it was, and was he ever surprised. It was a big black bear standing on his hind legs and eating garbage. The bear turned his head while still chewing and looked the watchman square in the face. The watchman threw his lantern down and ran as fast as you-know-what to get away from there.

Another time I was driving one of our boys to town in the camp pick-up truck to catch a bus for his home. Someone in his family was very ill. It was late at night and as we drove through Cherokee something came out of the darkness and ran across the road directly in front of me. It was a big black bear, and I mean big. I came within an inch of hitting it. Had I done so I would have wrecked that truck, probably totaling it. I don't know who was frightened the most, me or the bear. I would say, me.

Chapter Eleven

The Tree Climbers

Later my friend Stormy was assigned to work with me on the mechanic's job in the camp. We spent many happy days working together. One day we were assigned to patrol the telephone line from the camp up to Newfound Gap. The line was a single wire strung on poles and sometimes trees when available. Over a period of time tree limbs would fall across the line and partially ground it out. The line ran from our camp across the ridge and on to the park headquarters in Gatlinburg, Tennessee. Our job was to clear our side of the line.

We had climbers that strapped to our legs, a pair of pole climbers and a pair of tree climbers. Stormy wore the pole climbers and I had the tree climbers. I brought along the pair of radio headphones thinking that if I tied one wire to the climbers and the other to the line, I could listen in on the phone conversation. It didn't work. There was another thing that didn't work either. Never climb a pole with a pair of tree climbers. The tree climbers have longer spikes on them for penetrating the bark of the tree and going on into the solid wood. When using them on a pole, the longer spikes cause your legs to sit out at an angle and causes extra strain on them. I got half way up and gave out. I couldn't go up and I couldn't go down. What next? Slide down! Another thing, when wearing tree climbers never put your bare hands on the telephone line. You see, if someone rings the telephone at that time you are in for a shock because you are grounded by the tree. You learn a lot of things when you're in the C.C.C.

Chapter Twelve

Dangers Abounded

When working with trees one has to learn to be careful. One day a crew was working on a trail leading out from Newfound Gap and two of the guys cut down a tree. They had cut it high on the stump and the tree had fallen with a large splinter still holding. They proceeded to cut the splinter, one boy standing on each side and one standing with his back to a large cliff.

When the splinter was finally cut, one of the limbs trapped under the fallen tree had thrown it into a bind. When the splinter was finally cut, the tree swung around, pushing the boy on the cliffside backwards, causing him to fall onto the rocks below. He was severely injured.

The crew managed to get him back up onto the trail and then proceeded to make what we call a "boy scout stretcher." This is done by cutting two small poles and having two boys hold them at each end, one pole in each hand, and then slide their buttoned-up jackets off over their heads turning the sleeves wrong-side-out and down over the poles, thus creating a stretcher. They then carried him, running as fast as they could, back to Newfound Gap.

Arriving at Newfound Gap, they had no means of contacting the camp. The truck that brought them to the Gap that morning would not come back to pick them up until quitting time. There was a contractor building a road out to Clingman's Dome and one of his trucks happened to come by. The boys commandeered that truck and took the injured boy down to the camp about six miles away, where an ambulance was called to take him to the hospital. Unfortunately, the young man died.

On another occasion and at another location a crew was working out in the forest area when a tree was cut down and somehow fell on one of the boys, breaking his legs. Again a boy scout stretcher was rigged and two boys started running, carrying him back to the camp. Four boys started out running ahead of them. About halfway back to the camp two of them stopped, waited for the stretcher crew to arrive, and relieved them, continuing on with the stretcher. The other two ran on to the camp to report the accident and send two fresh guys back toward the site to meet the second stretcher crew and take over. After arriving at the camp the injured boy was taken by ambulance to the army hospital at Fort Oglethorpe, Georgia. He remained there many months before his legs healed properly and he was sent back to the camp. Many years later, long after we both had left the C.C.C., on my way to visit my hometown I would stop by to visit with him at a store he ran in Macon, North Carolina.

Chapter Thirteen

Upsetting Times

A memorable and quite disastrous event occurred while I was in the C.C.C.: the loss of the power shovel over the side of the mountain. It happened at the work site on the road to Newfound Gap, now U.S. Highway 441.

The operator was moving the shovel to a new work place and, in an attempt to change gears, the engine died while the transmission was in the neutral position. The shovel kept moving on its own and headed down a grade toward the shoulder of the road. The operator tried in vain to stop the shovel and could not. When it reached the shoulder and teetered over the edge the operator dived out. The shovel continued over the side of the mountain.

A truck driver, "T-Dump" Pearce, was sent with his truck back to the camp to report the accident. "T-Dump" was a name we had given him because he told us that he had once driven a Model T Ford dump truck. Not everybody believed him but we honored him with the name anyway. He kept that name for the rest of his life.

The camp superintendent, Mr. Rosser, came up to investigate the situation, and what a sight befell him. There, many feet down the side of the mountain, sat the shovel in an inverted position. Luckily the ground was mostly loose dirt that had been dumped over the side to build the overlook.

Mr. Rosser did not let the problem upset him and everyone admired him for that. He handled everything beautifully. A crew built a large wooden ramp that was placed in front of the shovel's caterpillar treads and extended up to the edge of the road. Two very large block and tackle sets were borrowed from somewhere to be attached, one to each side of the shovel. The only piece of machinery that we had available to use on the reclamation job was our caterpillar tractor with its power winch.

The power shovel being pulled up by two block and tackle sets.

The power shovel after it was pulled back up the mountain.

On the day the shovel was to be pulled back up the mountain everybody in camp, all except the cooks, turned out to help with the job. The tractor with its winch was tied to one block and tackle set and the men all pulled on the other set. That shovel was turned upright and pulled back up that mountain. One thing about those C.C.C. boys—they could pull together.

Once back on the road, workbenches were built and the job of repairing the shovel began. Many years later I revisited the park service garage and there was the old shovel, dents and all, just sitting there.

Chapter Fourteen

Food for Thought

The most popular building in camp was the mess hall. It was staffed by two teams of cooks who worked on alternate days with "K.P.'s" (Kitchen Police), of course. Their hours were from around four o'clock in the morning until eight o'clock in the evening. Since our electrical power plant had been shut down at ten o'clock the previous evening their first job was to start it again in the morning.

Early one morning, and I mean early, I was awakened by one of the cooks who asked me to go out and start the power plant. Knowing where my next meal was coming from, I, of course, complied. They had been unable to get the power going. The weather was very, very cold and they had flooded the engine with gasoline. I removed the spark plugs, squirted some oil in the cylinders to establish compression, and got the engine started and the electric lights working.

I walked back into the candle-lit kitchen and was greeted by a round of applause. I was told that I could have anything that I wanted to eat. I said, "How about some scrambled eggs?" The cook said, "How many do you want?" I said, "How many do you have?" I think I ate somewhere between a half and a whole dozen. For once in my life I was full.

Hanging just outside the mess hall door was a triangular shaped device made by bending a large steel rod. When the meal was ready a cook, using another piece of steel rod, would hammer on it and ring the chow call.

Every morning at breakfast on the table there would be a large pitcher of milk with small boxes of cereal for each place. Evidently some of the boys had never been served cereal. They treated it as

Standing outside the mess hall waiting for the dinner bell to be rung. Note the big metal triangle waiting to be struck.

The most popular building in camp was the mess hall. There were about twenty tables at which some two hundred men were served.

dessert and ate it last. But, if you ate yours first, as people normally do, when you reached for the ham and eggs there might not be any left. So some of us organized what we called "last table gang" and enjoyed our cereal first and then our ham and eggs. Also on each table, of course, there would be a large pitcher of coffee.

There were, I believe, about twenty tables in the mess hall. Some two hundred men were served. Near the exit from the mess hall stood a large screened-in box where the loaf bread was kept. Sometimes during the winter months, on our way out after the evening meal, one of us would snitch a loaf of bread and take it to the barracks where we would make toast on the wood stove that night.

The bread was delivered every other day by a truck from Asheville. Sometimes when a boy was going back home for any reason, he would hitch a ride to Asheville on the bread truck and take a bus from there. What do they say? "Bread is the staff of life."

Chapter Fifteen

Making Music

No doubt you've heard the words, "I like mountain music – good old mountain music – played by a real hillbilly band." Well, we had just that. Coon Hunter Day would have all the boys that could play a musical instrument get together with him several nights a week in the foreman's quarters. We had a few boys in camp that had brought their guitars, mandolins, and banjos from home. They were quite good players.

Coon Hunter would place them in a circle around him and proceed to tune up. He would have his straw boss Harvey sit in the back of the room and back him up. Coon Hunter, aside from being the champion coon hunter of Tennessee, was probably also the champion fiddle player. He would say to one musician, "Sound your A" and the boy would sound his A, and then Coon Hunter would say, "How does that sound, Harvey?" Harvey would say, "Sounds good, Mr. Day."

This action would be repeated for every musician in the room and each time Harvey's answer would be the same, "Sounds good, Mr. Day." I had never heard of Harvey disagreeing with Coon Hunter on anything. After they were all tuned up, Coon Hunter would put his fiddle in place, pat his foot three times, and say, "Aye, God, boys, let her go." Then came "Coming Round the Mountain," "Leather Britches," and all those old tunes. Yes sir, they were played by a real hillbilly band.

Many years later, while at a hardware store near my home in Norfolk, Virginia, I ran into a man by the name of Tabor. I said, "You wouldn't happen to know a person called Harve Tabor, would you? He said, "Of course, he's my father. He lives with me now."

I said, "Well, I'll be dammed!" and that opened a new door. I visited old Harve and we reminisced those good old days.

One of the boys in our barracks wanted to be in Coon Hunter's band. He had a mandolin which he would sit and pick every night. However, he never seemed to improve. We finally took up a collection to buy the mandolin. Our plan was to purchase the mandolin and then throw it away. However, the boy discovered our plan and refused to sell it, but he did improve his musical ability.

Chapter Sixteen

Feeling at Home

Another important building in camp was the latrine. It was our combination outhouse, shower, bath and washroom. It was manned by one of the boys known as the "latrine orderly". In the latrine was a Maytag washing machine that was gasoline driven. The latrine guy would wash our clothes for us for a few cents each month. What the heck! He wasn't going anywhere and he had the time. Once our clothes were washed, we would spread them out on bushes or anywhere to keep them off the ground while they dried.

I also had the job of keeping the washing machine motor running. It was a very small two-cycle engine. One day when I had the engine removed, I started it, held it in my lap, and sat down in a wheelbarrow. Another guy pushed me and the wheelbarrow through the camp. We pretended the washing machine motor was

Frank Davis strolling through camp.

running the wheelbarrow. As we passed the officers' quarters, the captain came out the door, saw us and broke into a big belly laugh.

What the hell, fun is fun no matter how you come by it.

Chapter Seventeen

Mechanic Memories

For the latter part of my tour in the C.C.C., I was assigned to the National Park Service Garage in Smokemont, North Carolina. It had been built on the grounds of a camp there about four miles from my camp. I was taken back and forth each workday by pickup truck.

This large garage did the overhaul and repair of all trucks and equipment in the area. It was staffed with the superintendent, two mechanics, and two C.C.C. boys—me and another boy from the adjacent camp.

The garage had its own electrical power supply consisting of a large 110-volt DC electrical generator powered by a standard Chevrolet truck engine. The engine was equipped with a governor that kept it running at a constant speed throughout the working day.

In the beginning there was a problem with engine cooling. Many systems were tried, but finally we wound up with a standard truck radiator. But to be sure, we ran a pipe out to a nearby stream and kept a constant supply of fresh water running to the radiator and, of course, a constant drain.

The generator was located in a little powerhouse built next to the garage. Every morning someone would have to go out and start the system for the day.

The two park service mechanics took me under their wing. As a result, I became experienced in many things while there. I overhauled engines, transmissions, brake systems, repaired truck bodies, and many other things. I even learned to weld. My number one tutor was a fellow called "Red" Farmer. He was in the U.S. Army Air Force during World War I. Years later, when my wife and I were revisiting the area, we stopped by to see Red and his wife and spent the night with them.

Each day I brought my lunch with me to work in a little brown bag. The other C.C.C. boy would bring a big pot of coffee, tea, or whatever they were having at his mess hall that day. Working men have to eat, do they not?

The creek next to the shop was dammed up to make a swimming hole. Just before the opening of the trout season, the pool would be filled with trout. We would take a fishing rod out and catch a few. We would bring them into the shop and put them in the large water tank that we used for testing radiators. They would swim around for the rest of the day while we went back to work.

Since it was out of season, at the end of the workday we would net them, take them back to the creek, and throw them in. Fish also deserve a little extracurricular activity!

Those were my best days. The experience I gained while working at the garage stood me well for many years to come as a career was being built for me.

Chapter Eighteen

A Night On The Town

On some Friday and Saturday nights the camp would send trucks into the neighboring towns of Sylva and Bryson City to give the boys a night out. We could go to a movie, date a girl, or do whatever we could find to do, but women always come first – everybody knows that. There might be as many as twenty-five or thirty of us in the back of a truck. We would sing songs as we rode down the mountain – songs like "Will the Circle Be Unbroken." I can still hear that truckload of boys stomping their feet and singing.

The truck would leave for the return trip to camp around 10:30 p.m. If you were not there on time to catch it, you were left behind. This happened to quite a few guys at one time or another. It wasn't the worst thing in the world. For the next day was never a workday. Thank goodness we didn't have to answer to roll calls.

One Friday night two other boys and I missed the truck and were left stranded in town. Walking down the street, figuring what to do next, we passed a small hotel. No one was on duty at that late hour but it didn't matter because we couldn't have afforded a room anyway.

We looked through the window and noticed two big easy chairs and a long comfortable looking sofa just sitting there with nobody in them. We tried the door and it wasn't locked. We slipped inside and stretched out. We were asleep in nothing flat. One boy slept too well. He snored so loud that he woke the woman who ran the place. She came in and told us that we could not sleep in her lobby. We told her our story and she said, "Well, I've got a room upstairs in which someone left a window open, and it rained in on one side of the bed. You can have that room for free if you want it."

We took the room, of course, and made the boy who did the snoring sleep on the wet side. When we woke the next morning he was gone.

Suddenly there was a loud knock on the door. When we opened it, there stood the hotel lady and she was as mad as an old wet hen. She said, "Someone went into one of my other rooms and slept in the bed, leaving it a mess!" We pleaded innocent, knowing full well who it likely was.

When we got back down on the street Saturday morning, we saw the snorer and told him that the hotel lady was going to have him picked up. We had fabricated the story, of course, but when he saw the one and only policeman in town he said to him, "If that hotel woman comes to you and says anything about me, it's not so." The policeman had no idea what the boy was talking about and that ended that. But you can bet your bottom dollar, we did not miss the truck back to camp on another Friday night.

Frank Davis beside one of the trucks used to transport the CCC boys to Sylva or Bryson City for rest, relaxation, and recreation.

Chapter Nineteen

In Closing

When any of you visit the Great Smoky Mountains National Park, I hope you enjoy it as much as we C.C.C. boys enjoyed helping build it.

The days that I spent in the Civilian Conservation Corps were without a doubt the best and the most important days of my life. I became acquainted with some of the finest people on earth, people that otherwise I would never have known, and I married the girl I dated in Sylva. I owe it all to one of the greatest presidents this country has ever known, Franklin D. Roosevelt.

All the enclosed are old memories of younger days and may be slightly eroded with age. If so, please excuse.

Frank Davis, 2005

Elizabeth Sherrill, the young woman he met while in the C.C.C. camp, and who he later married.

Frank Davis (right) and some of his C.C.C. friends.

Frank standing beside a truck in front of the camp office.

CPSIA information can be obtained
at www.ICGtesting.com
Printed in the USA
JSHW040235170622
27046JS00002B/4